The Making of
Aaliyah Zakat

The Making of
Aaliyah Zakat

Aaliyah Zakat

BALBOA.
PRESS

A DIVISION OF HAY HOUSE

ISBN: 978-1-4525-5051-0 (sc)
ISBN: 978-1-4525-5050-3 (e)

Balboa Press books may be ordered through booksellers or by contacting:

Balboa Press
A Division of Hay House
1663 Liberty Drive
Bloomington, IN 47403
www.balboapress.com
1-(877) 407-4847

Because of the dynamic nature of the Internet, any web addresses or links contained in this book may have changed since publication and may no longer be valid. The views expressed in this work are solely those of the author and do not necessarily reflect the views of the publisher, and the publisher hereby disclaims any responsibility for them.

The author of this book does not dispense medical advice or prescribe the use of any technique as a form of treatment for physical, emotional, or medical problems without the advice of a physician, either directly or indirectly. The intent of the author is only to offer information of a general nature to help you in your quest for emotional and spiritual well-being. In the event you use any of the information in this book for yourself, which is your constitutional right, the author and the publisher assume no responsibility for your actions.

Any people depicted in stock imagery provided by Thinkstock are models, and such images are being used for illustrative purposes only.
Certain stock imagery © Thinkstock.

Printed in the United States of America

Balboa Press rev. date: 4/23/2012

DEDICATION: JFA BOOK

This book was inspired from the love a mother have for her child. The love to not want or need for a child to experience rights abuse, sexual abuse, discrimination, harassment, and threats that stop freedom liberties and Justice for All. I dedicate this book to you child of God that God sent you from a special place to do specials works for Him. I respect that and I respect your Gift of life , So thats why I sought to prepare a safe and secure future with you in mind. Always praise God and turn to God for peace and love in this world. May God bless you to always believe in him and believe in yourself.

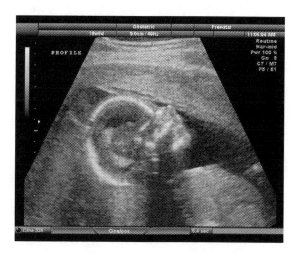

THE HOUSE OF SECRETS

Growing up in Philadelphia born and raised would apply to my life.Yes I totally identify with the theme music Fresh Prince of bel Air. Only thing I never made it to Bel Air and with a father so strict I never really much played outdoors. I remember a family that would appeal to most having the presence of both parents. However things that can look Pretty is not always what it seems. Growing up I never had a relationship with my father that I would consider to be healthy. Me and my siblings was basically programmed to fear my father by the force of his words which lead to the force of his big belt. My father lived upstairs in the house I knew as home he would mainly go to work or when he was home he would make sure we was always working. It did not matter if it was school the next day sometimes me and my siblings was kept home to finish cleaning for the next day. My Father always love to flex his powers in any way to mark his role in the house to me and my siblings. My Mother being the calm one in the house was the total opposite from my father she always made sure we had food, and always added that balance in the house for the sanity that we needed. My Mother had six children ,four by my father and two of my siblings was from previous relationships. I always loved the comfort having my brothers and cousins around.

Being the youngest felt good growing up However apart of me yearned to be older like my siblings. I would see my cousin go out and she had lots of friends that would recognized her. Around that time all I wanted to be recognized and popular. All I wanted to feel special in my own way and feel loved by everyone. I always wore my cousin clothes my cousin being four years older than me we was not quite the same size. I was around a size two in jeans and I never knew .To keep my cousin jeans from falling off my petite frame I would role the waist of the pants several times to prevent a wardrobe malfunction. I had some associates while I was in Elementary school .Being in such a strict environment as a child I did not know just how to be a normal child, everything in my house was restricted that just being a child playing with other children was vague to me. I always was a loner outside of my house. I had a few associates in school and in my neighborhood I played sometimes with the next door neighbors mostly when my father was working. If he would be home most of the time that meant being in the house. I just remember me being a little girl with such s big heart. I just wanted love and I wanted to love every body. Often I would see so much of mistreatment done to different people around me .I could never understand Why would a human Being want to hurt another Human being. To me it was strange for me to witness such unexplained actions. Often I would feel a need to reach out. However parts of me being overly shy never feeling surety of me as a person. While I was a child my imagination ran wild. It always took me some where new and exciting. As I can remember I made up all types of games. I recall playing wheelof fortune not no store bought game it was home made. Me being extremely artistic sometimes had a down side when I was the only person interested. Creativity always was going on in my life. .Masking my feelings of insecurities would be the reason to not intervined. Having the presence of my siblings going to the same Elementary School Charles Richard Drew Elementary School was the days. With my siblings being older and attending school with me was so cool being so young and unsure. The presence of may siblings made me feel like everything was okay. Despite my shyness I was always on honor roll . I knew I was a bright person inside and out. My elementary days was the best aside from my brothers being jumped going to school every week. We would never know any of the boyz, but they sure acted as if they knew us. They would rush my brothers and strart punching and jumping on them. I always was put in situations that made me feel defenseless. Afterwards it was just like another school day, we would continue are walk to school. I often felt like I just seen everything cause I would never say anything or do anything .I was around 7 years old when my brothers was being bullied. Even though I never express words or actions I always hanged on to the sadness and hurt they may have felt being victims to such violence. All my life I feel like I just held information and I could never tell anyone. So as my brothers had got older and they began to graduate the school that I would to graduate someday too. I was happy for them because apart of me wanted the bullying to be over and in my young mind I figured if they don't have to go that way to get to school then they won't be hurt. I loved all my siblings . Sad to say the bullying may have been over outside,however it began to enter in the place I called home. I never no why but apart of me would just get angry at my cousin and I would just hit her. Soon that bullying seized.

However my mid aged brother would bully my youngest brother I was the peacemaker. I would often have to witness my youngest brother crying and sad. I would see him in the hallway crying his little eyes out and I would feel so furiated that someone could make him feel this way. No longer would I associate my self with my mid age brother. He was then like a enemy to me. I took my youngest brother under my wing . I cared about him so much. I never wanted nothing to happen to him. It was certain that he was safe with me always. With the two of them sharing a room, sometimes he was not always by my side. I t seemed that any time he was not near me my mid age brother was bothering him. It often seemed that he would wait for me to be absent to make him cry. It never matter I would run always to him. There was a particular incident that I would never forget. Both of my brothers was in there room when I hear screaming and my youngest brother is crying so loud I ran to go in the room to save him from what was going on when I turned the knob it was locked I began to panic .I just knew that he was hurting him . Afterwards he came out the room crying. I was screaming at my mid age brother to leave him alone and don't bother him any more. Till this day I will not no what took place behind the lock door, just the memory makes me cry. This will be another one of my painful childhood memories. Very often I remember me and my siblings always getting beatings when we were children. For reasons that was simply unexplainable. If he heard us playing because we could not go outside he was so upset. There was an incident that happened between my brothers and my father and the police were called to the house. Me and my siblings was relieved that once in are entire time being in that house it felt like we had the victory for. While time was passing we were all getting older. So even though my parents was fortunate to stay together for several years. Me and my siblings all was familiar with the problems that was between them. Mabye we did not know exactly why, but we knew they had issues. I mean it was round the clock drama. It was so disgraceful to see to people supposedly your parents fighting and arguing on a daily basis. In all actuality I was pretty surprise that the marriage lasted how long that it did. Forgive me for be honest, but the truth is the truth. When things where boiling down to the ultimate breaker which was a divorce. It was like when you know something is coming, But you don't know when. I mean that marriage was miserable. Me and my siblings was miserable the my parents was miserable and I did not know for what. The part that always puzzled me was why can't everyone just get along. It sounds easier than I guess the actual demonstration. In my family we practice Islam. We definitely had the obedience. Thanks to my father, However there was not enough love. As said in the bible how can a person say they love God when they can't even love there brother or cousin that they see every day. To me it always seemed that it was so easy to find and know the answers. But people made it so difficult. Because of my shyness I would keep so much to myself. I had such a hard time opening up. Me expressing my feelings was sort of like an extinct thing. While growing up I had solutions in me I just never knew how to implement the solutions. When growing up it seemed that God filled me with so much knowledge so much wisdom, but took away my voice. It was a challenge so much for me to express what was really on my mind. It was such a difficult challenge that seemed to come easy with others.

Well I was reaching a period of my life where things was turning around for everyone in my family. My cousin was in High School and my brother was in High School . My oldest brother was getting ready to graduate. Soon I would be looking forward to High School this was the moment it seemed I waited for all my life. I actually dreamed of this moment. Finally the time was approaching for me to experience what I been waiting for. Well when my oldest brother graduated he began to work and he was preparing for his future. All I really remember that he was focused on working. As time went on he was set on venturing off to be independent. So he eventually brought a house. I was still young but I knew that time was moving and everybody in are family had different agendas. So when my brother finally moved out I was fortunate to have his room. I was so happy. Also so I was experiencing the life I had my own room. Finally it was so good. My cousin on the other hand had her party life. It seemed she was more gone than ever. She had a girl that she consider her best friend, so as she enjoyed hanging out I was left to be by myself. My cousin and mother would get in to disagreements. My cousin wanted to hang out or spend the night out so they would disagree about them issues. GROWING up with my cousin was my comfort; I always looked up to her. I loved her so much I always admired her. My cousin lifestyle was so appealing to me. She was like the it girl when we was growing up. She always had friends always had nice clothes and was admired by all the people. From elementary school my cousin carried her popularity on. I think growing up I always wanted to experienced a little of her life. When my cousin began High School, I was still in elementary school. I felt like my life was always boring. I just wanted to feel popular

I wanted all the guys to know my name. I wanted my cousin life. Soon I would find out that what Glitter is not gold. Soon I will find out that love starts with God and yourself. Loving the person God bless you to be. I would soon have to find out the hard way. My cousin made High School seem like a vacation, she was acquainted with people that had cars. Then she had Girlfriends, one particular girl she always hung around named Ida. My cousin knew Ida home as a second home. I grew more close to my youngest Brother we would join each other in every thing that we would do. While my cousin was gone a lot I found other interest. I started growing close with a girl that I went to school with and she lived right around the corner .We begun to hang out every day. I started to feel like somebody. I felt alive I felt like I was starting to love my life. The girl that lived around the corner from me also hung out with another girl, so we three would hang out and enjoy each other company. We would try to find places to go here and there. We never knew all of the hot spots. As long as we were out of the house or away from the neighborhood, we were cool. Therefore, my cousin had her life and I had been developing my life. Then something had come out about my cousin. My cousin was supposedly pregnant. Even though those things was not talked about. Because of my father being so strict they was like no, no's without any thing ever being said about sex or pregnancy. Therefore, my cousin soon was taking to the doctor to get an abortion. From the point on all hell was breaking loose. My cousin had a breakdown. The cousin I always looked up to was crumbling right before my eyes. I felt helpless; I always wanted to be like this person, how I could help. The nice clothes the friend magnet the popular cousin I once known was gone. My cousin would have so many attacks she break all the walls in the house. My mother and my cousin would be fighting she would scream and curse all over the house. It was a madhouse .All this time my fixation on her life when it must have been something just trying to keep it all together. Soon my cousin breakdowns had become so intense that she went away for likes a year. Soon I felt so alone the person I looked up to all my life was gone. There were nights I cried I would just stay up and cry. Growing up I never express myself we never talked about are feeling. Therefore, the feelings I felt all I knew was to cry. I would cry a lot at night. I always felt that I needed my cousin for me to know who I was. I guess when you always wore a person clothes always wanted the life of someone else's and always wanted to feel like someone when that person is gone you really never knew yourself and the person you thought you knew you find out they no longer exist. My life was all over the place I felt I needed to shape my life on any and everything I ever known. I started rebelling I wanted the streets and the streets wanted me. I felt depressed crying with no one to dry my tears no one to hold me I knew that I was yearning for something I missed my cousin. I began hanging out with my friend that lived around the corner with me anywhere she was I was. However, the pain I kept inside was still there and the quick fix was only temporary. I was staying out sometimes until 2:00am on a school day. All of my actions were SO WHAT. I would carry my behavior on in school arguing with my teachers. I was hurting and no one knew the pain I could not even talk about it. My mother told me if someone ask you about where is your cousin or wanting to know what happened just say I do not know. I did exactly that, however I was still masking my own hurts behind the situation. Soon my 8th grade graduation was approaching. Soon, later I was getting ready for Graduation. It was finally my time the baby of all of my siblings. I was finally on my way. I was so happy my graduating class was so close. We all looked at one another as a family. I could not asked for a better Graduating class. My graduation day was so memorable. My outfit was like last minute, however I looked so cute. When I arrived to my graduation my classmates did not even recognize me. All I heard was " Aaliyah " Aaliyah is that you. I felt great, things could not have felt better. This shy girl with a caring big heart was growing up. It was my time and I was shining. My classmates was so use to seeing me with baggy jeans and big shirts thanks to my cousin for her {Hand me Downs}. It was a shock to see me in a form fitting dress that showed off my real size. I was really a size two I women pants, but I was always wearing a size 10 which was what my cousin wore. I never really made any complaints in ways I was happy to wear her clothes. I never realized that her clothes made me look bigger than I actually was. So here I was and there was all my classmates. We was finally saying good bye . We where starting a new chapter. We all laughed together some even cryed together. It was so beautiful. I did it, we all did it. Now I could enjoy the summer and get ready for High School. Yes I was finally going to be a Freshman in High School. I was saying good bye to Elementary School and I was saying hello to High School. Now I had the summer to recap on elementary school and prepare for High School. I spent my summer in the streets. In my neighborhood was really nothing productive to do. We as kids in the neighborhood had to find things to do. Well I spent most of my time with a girl I graduated Elementary School with. This girl lived right around the corner from me. It was so convenient, to have a so one I knew around the corner from me. I would get up every morning and go around her house. It was like a daily ritual for me. For the majority of my childhood I never had a lot of associates. If I had one or two buddies I would want to be close forever. In my younger years it was like that. There was something inside of me that yearned for excitement. I really never fill that part in me. So in my young mind I look for things only that was self destructive for me. The only things I remember doing is going back and forth to the store, listening to music and eating. As these few things became just the normal thing to look forward to. After that what followed was the attraction for guys in the neighborhood.

LASH OUT

I was so happy to see all of my classmates; however, I was ready for the next chapter of my life. I was yearning for something new. The time was now for a new beginning for me. All and All everything I experience during Elementary School I was ready to put all behind me and start fresh I was ready for my summer of 1998 and preparing for the new chapter of my life. My lifestyle still involved me hanging in the streets. While doing so this guy would always try to approach me from what I understood he had the same religion as me. Therefore, I felt a sense of familiarity and he was supposedly friends of my cousin. Every time he would see me, he always spoke. Sometimes a little innocent flirting. The absence of my cousin made me yearn for any thing that reminded me of her. What seemed to be the perfect thing turned out only to be a nightmare? This person always seemed to be around. I knew if I was in the streets that I would see him. So I would make sure that I would be around. The first time he invited me into his house I did not even think twice I said okay. I felt good in his presence. It felt like the void that I felt was filled. We sat on the bed talked briefly then soon he kissed me. It felt so good I started feeling valued I felt special. On a couple of other occasions we kissed and grinded with one another. This was the summer of my cousin returning home. I was excited however, I felt like I was in deep with this person that she knew, but I was getting to know. The arrival of my cousin made me want to stop everything between me and this person and focus on the love I have for my cousin. So I said to myself no more. My cousin was home I was going to be starting High School I was thrilled. I knew my cousin was home, but I could not shake a lifestyle I adapted to. I remember like yesterday me and my siblings was all in the room glad of my cousin presence, I was eager to get out of the house, but I made up in my mind that I was done with the foolishness. I honestly said I 'all be back I wanted to go to the store and get candy. On my way to the store the same guy chased me down, all over me hugging me, he was trying to kiss all over me. He got me to go to house by saying he has money for me that I would lend him. Arriving to a house I sat on the edge of the bed letting him gather the money, the money that I thought would be given to me. He began walking towards me pushing me down on the bed, holding my neck as he started to pull down my pants. I could not believe what was happening. A person that gained my trust was throwing it away right before my eyes. Every time I would lift up, he would hold my neck pushing me back down. He began to rape me. I did not know that someone I started to care about could ever do this to me. After the rape, I rushed home feeling dirty, First thing I did was get in the shower, scrubbing, and scrubbing myself. I knew what happened was wrong I guess I thought scrubbing myself would rid me of it all. I carried on as nothing ever happened to me. Soon I would be haunted by what happened. I tried to focus on me attending high school and that is it. I began to feel exhausted, and then

I started feeling symptoms of itching and burning feelings in my vagina. I knew that I never felt like this before. I knew of a clinic so I scheduled an appointment. I was so nervous. I knew I needed help it was like a different type of help. That was not the end of the symptoms I experienced. After receiving antibiotics, I was instructed to take all the pills. Therefore, I did exactly that. Once that finishing of the antibiotics. I started to experience itching on my vagina skin. Which soon I would be told by the doctor that they were warts. Here I was, it was another blow. It was like three knockouts your out. First with the violation of being rape. Then a diagnosis of one STD then here comes something else. From this point on I was done. I did not know what hit me. However, it took me down hard. Here I was feeling alone again. I told my cousin only to feel even more alone and isolated. I told my cousin that I was raped by Whalib and he gave me something. My cousin took that information and ran with it she scheduled a family meeting. That I did not know of until the day of. I already was dealing with a lot dealing what went down then to have to look at all of my brothers and cousin and mother face when my cousin just tell everybody with no hesitation. She says Aaliyah was raped leaving everybody face in shock. I was wordless; embarrass ashamed, I felt running and hiding forever. Now I was the outcast of the family. Afterwards everything was different my childhood was over. I would begin to be isolated and shut down. Everything I was anticipating high School to be like did not even matter to me any more. Life it self begin to feel as a nightmare. And I just wanted it to be over. I tried to embrace high school only to grow deeper in to a depression. The more I tried to hide the pain the more I hurtled. Everything I strived for had no more of a meaning to me. All through elementary school, I remember being an honor roll student. Now while in High School I was a under achiever. For some reason I could not seem to pull it together. I was lost I had no direction I had no drive, life seem as if no joy was present. All I felt was heartache. Because of these emotions, everything with me suffered. I wanted to do better, I did not know how to. The pressure of my past was weighing in so heavy on me I could not escape it. I was haunted everyday by what happened to me. Not only was I challenged by the Sexually Transmitted Disease I was challenged with blaming myself. I was left feeling so stupid for being so naïve. I felt so alone, so afraid, so confuse and so used.It was like I fell in to a deep and lonely pit. I suffered for years with all these negative emotions. In school all my work did nothing but produce discouraging grades and more of a depression. I had no one to talk to, I guess my relationship with God was buried to. At times I always called on God , However I still was very challenged.

WORKING THE POSTALYARD

This is where it all began at 30th St. the place most call the PO short for the place I would soon know as the graveyard. It all began early Jan 2002 I had my first real job working for the infamous Post Office. Nothing could prepare me for this rollercoaster that just kept throwing me off the ride. All I know that I wanted to do a good job. So my plan on doing a good job included me focused on work and not play. My fellow co-workers had cliques however I knew I was not there for that. Sometimes when we would break after standing for hours which seem like 1 hour multiplied to tired of standing .I would spend my breaks sometimes talking to a fellow co-worker Sashy. She was pretty talkative so she did not care who she talked to. I was pretty quiet on the work floor. I always followed directions. I just always wanted to do a good job. I was treated unfairly because I was not apart of the in crowd that did less work but more lolly gagging. On Several occasions I was harassed by my supervisors. There was one specific supervisor that always harassed me his name was Mr. Larry. On so many ocassions he would come over in my work area and make remarks of me doing a better job or me working faster. However he did not follow all his supervising duties correctly. On many occasions he would be around me and my co-workers area and he would be conversating, laughing and eating as if we where at a party rather on the work floor. There was so many incidents of harassment abuse injustices taken place on a daily basis. I consider these people as Adults with authority and I viewed myself as a honest employee just doing my job. On one occasion a supervisor named Mr. Lenn put me on a assignment for 3 to 4 people to do by myself. Then I was placed on another assignment after that with six big containers of mail. Then Supervisor Mr. Larry came over telling me to hurry and finish the mail. After finishing the mail It was time for my lunch, usually at lunch I would just relax and chill in the woman bathroom because the woman locker room is attached. I returned on time only to be put on another assignment by myself. There was no co-workers in sight this was a usual thing for the others to be M.I.A. and nothing done.I had no problem with any of my co-workers. I had a problem with the supervisors and there lack of supervising skills. I don't think it is that big of a crime to take more time then given when you have a break or lunch. All I'm saying is Justice for All. If I even dared to come back 2 to 3 minutes late I was threatened with suspension or termination. On Jan 4 2002 While I was into work at approximately 11:15pm to hit the clock Mr. Tart another Supervisor that mannerism was like Queer eye for the straight guy, but I was no guy and he was just as a jerk like the others. He approached me after hitting the clock saying"don't you think you're late. In comparison to my co-worker arriving on the floor around 11:40pm and nothing was said.The next day Jan 5 we are scheduled on the floor at 5:45. I returned when the others took there usual 15 to 20 minutes extra. Like the same song different day. I was going into my bag for a pair of gloves when a supervisor Mr. Larry hollering get to work. Right next to me my co-worker was eating and nothing was said. On one occasion I was asked to do a assignment at the time my lunch was approaching. I started the assignment with a co –worker named jamal only to be left there by my self to finish his assignment and mines. I began to see how wrong people are. I never knew people could be so evil. I learned fast just how evil people could be and was. The mask of injustices that was the uncovered lie of the rest of the deceptions of the United States Post Office.

WHO'S THE MENTAL PATIENT

It all started after the completion of my nursing aide program. I began my search for a job. I had no experience working in the field of nursing assistant. All I knew is that I had my certification I just needed and wanted a job. After working for an agency where they want you to go to clients house and provide care on a one on one basis. I yearned for more of a challenge applying my skills that I learned in a steady environment. I was in for a road ahead that may have been steady but far from stabile. Frustration grew with the feelings of under achievements. I knew that I needed more. With my daughter being born she was my hope and I was hers. I couldn't stand to look at my beautiful child of God and feel incompetent of providing her with a beautiful life. To only match who God bless her to be. Just the thought of it was a daily disturbance. I found myself daydreaming of how was it going to come together. I briefly had to work at the Post office two months after my daughter birth. I knew that I just had a baby also I knew I needed money to raised this baby. With determination stirring in my insides to stand for whatever. I felt strong, but I was submissive. I knew I did not want to work at the Post Office however I knew that I wasn't fulfilled financially. So I bit the bullet and said here I am. Included was a long drawn out orientation just to work back at a dungeon. Once I officially started working back at the post office I was so focused on doing my job being cordial getting payed and doing it all over. The fact I was now a Certified nursing assistant I still yearned for that job in that areana. So while working as a Postal employee I still made time to search for a job as a CNA. I was on my grind knowing that I was not going to stop. With hearing people that was working as CNA say how much either they made to telling me how much this place is paying to how much this place is paying. Just hearing them stories had me excited. I wanted it so I did every and anything to assure that I would one day get it. So I was constantly going in person putting in my applications that they had to make the process electronically. I was determined I posted my resume. Suddenly I would be shocked to hear from a job in Warminister, Pa miles from where I was from. However I was relieved, happy and desperate at the same time. Here was my opportunity. Here it was a chance for me. I called immediately setting up an interview. The interview went great .Something let me know they needed CNA'S and I wanted a job that needed CNA'S. It was perfect I knew I was saying good- bye to the Post Office and I was saying hello to what I worked for. I did everything I had to get physicals, vaccinations more long orientations. However I was here. I completed everything just so I could guarantee me a job. My excitement for this job was on over drive I was eager to get on that work floor and put these skills I learned to work. I began working for this nursing home July 2007. In half of the training I was to basically watch everything the girl that was training me. And assist with care for the residents. The second half of training was more than I could ever imagine happening .Me and the girl agreed that I would help out as much as I could without us working side by side. So we did just that It was supper time, so we agreed that I would assist with the care for the Bed feedings residents that eat in bed. I prepared everything as I learned propping his head and lifting the head of his bed to a eating position. Everything was going great he was eating. Finishing all his food I then let him relax and took the food tray away. Soon after hearing the nurse that was on duty shouting who fed Mr. Bruce knowing I fed him rushing in the room. Mr bruce room walls and bed filled with vomit. Mr. Bruce regurtated all his food. The nurse Denemy repeatedly saying what happened what happened. I told everything that happened as far as feeding him however come to find out when in that position he had special pillows to keep him aligned I did not know. The girl that was training me knew but she never made sure that I knew or that they was applied. So now the nurse is saying I could lost my certification if he would have died, saying he could have died. In my mind I'm thinking I did not even get started and I 'm about to lose my CNA certification, this job and may have to testify in court. I'm now feeling like maybe I should have stayed at the post office. So after everything is cleaned the Nurse Denemy shifts the blame on the girl saying what she should have done. Only a week into it and I started feeling like what did I get myself into. After my week of training on the actual work floor I did not know if I should throw in the towel or go through the fire. I chose to go through the fire The beginning of my days at this nursing home would prove to be tiresome. I was driving a hour to get there and caring for 8 residents a night. I was exhausted by time I got there. I never let that stop me for providing a 100% care to the residents. I was also working on what was considered to be the most challenging floor. The dementia, mentally impaired unit. I wanted a challenge I wasn't aware that it would be so mentally challenging. Feeling like I was in a whole another world. I was committed so I knew that I was here, here to stay. On my shift there was only 4 CNA's on duty they was under staff. Every CNA had a number of 8-10 residents a night. Wow it was like being superwoman. Without the super powers and cape. The lack of staff and the mentally challenged residents was a weary situation. I knew that one thing all understand is love. And I am a firm believer that love is the universal language and know matter what race, mental or physical impairments we have. We want and need love. So with my understandment of God and what God requires of me and others I came to that job everyday on time ready to work because of that reason alone. I finally had my own assignment of residents I was responsible for. I was excited that I could build a friendship with my residents and do my job. There was one catch because I was the new girl I was left with the assignment no one wanted to do. I did not care I was just ready for whatever. These residents was not mobile and most of all the residents weighed over 200 lbs. That was trouble because everything I had to do for my residents two sometimes three people had to assist. Okay if there only four CNA'S and close to 40 residents how is this going to work. There began a lot of problems with people wanting to help to basically no one wanted to help no one especially the new person. Which was me. I became the person that no one wanted to help. I would literally have to beg someone to assist me. It was clear to me that these people was not here for the residents. There no way a person they could care if they do not care for the well being of every last person in this Nursing Home that needs help. I always was a help to any that would need my assistance. It was already bad enough being responsible for 8-10 residents a night. That including feeding, bathing, and checking every so often with incontinence clean ups. However I was focus on getting the job done with lowsy assistance. Also it did not help any with one particular residence that love to play with her feces. On several occasions I arrived in her room only to see her covered with feces. I would have to clean her up along with cleaning all her sheets and covers. However when I would leave she would only do it again. I witness her literally looking in her anus to find feces. It was a nightmare, a nightmare that stinked. So when she would get up for dinner I felt as though she should be the last resident to be put to bed. This solution proven to work. The nurse on duty for that side of the nursing home known as the Denemy had a problem with the solution. But when it was a problem she acted helpless. So it was now a solution and she did not want me to make her my last resident to be put to bed. How ridiculous. I always felt like she was so idiotic. On a particular day she basically tried to write me up about the matter. Everything about her was so fake and ignorant she was like a living devil in the flesh. I basically explained to her that putting her in early only allows her to have more time for a FECEStival. And Denemy was not going to step in and help with the clean-up. However she had everything to say about what should be done. Personally she had a problem with me. For what I didn't know quite frankly I did not care. I just did not need to be harassed while caring for 10 residents a night with no one that wants to help. This place was so mismanaged and I was ready to move on. My fellow co-workers was bitter the nurse on duty was bitter the residents just knew that they had to be there. It all started to wear on me the long day to night and repeating it day after day after day. Not only was I dealing with drama at work, I was also going home and being irritated with my child father. While I was at work he would watch our daughter. I was so thankful however sometimes I wish it was reversed. He had no idea the headache I had to endure everyday. Yes it was everyday. On the 11th of Nov 2007 while working that day I was responsible for giving one of my residents a shower. This resident was so pyranoid. All I would do for her is calm her down every time she would panic. However she did not even calm down, she just started trippin even more. So I was then just focused on getting her shower done. So I began to get her ready for her shower. As she get in the shower room everything was fine. Then the Nurse Denemy storms in the bath room screaming telling me that I have something else to do. I calmly told her that I am going to finish caring for my resident that I was caring for before she stormed in the bathroom . So she seemed to be upset, She left out the bathroom screaming I don't want to hear her bullshit. I was so disrespected and everybody on the unit heard her. Everybody was just cool with her being disrespectful and mean for no reason. Plenty of her days she spent making things difficult.I could not understand why we all just could not get along. I was pretty much use to injustice. It change the fact that I was sick of it. It seemed everyday I had to have my guard up. I did not know what angle Ms. Denemy was coming from day from day. My days was so frustrating having to see her face, and do my job. I knew that my time was approaching for me to find another job. I could not help but to think how hard it took me to find a job. It had to be something better than this.

BACK TO THE GRAVEYARD

Well here I was again I had enough of this Nursing Home aka Mental Institution I needed an escape. Here I was preparing myself for an opening position at the Post Office. The only thing I would be a carrier this time around. I just knew this would be different. I thought it would be in a good way until I was shown other wise. First thing I had another orientation long and boring. Then we had to go to driving academy. Then I had to pass the driving course. Well I pass everything alright. It seemed like I was in some type of boot camp or something all this for a job that is not giving benefits and is not a career. I was still determine to do what I had to do. The only good thing I seen that my work location was my neighborhood Post office. I was thrilled about that, comparing it to the stories I previously heard about other workers being sent to others facilities far from where they live. Before arriving, I was told on the phone that I would meet with the manager. So arriving I was prepared for my meeting with the manager Mr. Taliban. When I arrived I asked for Mr. Taliban, While waiting I started to think about my work history with the post office. I started thinking about all the ancient people working there that gave twenty even thirty years of there life. I felt sad I felt like apart of the crew, But I'm only 22 years old. While waiting at the same time I wanted to run out the doors for my dear life. However I couldn't I walked in with to much determination to achieve. I couldn't run I was back at the graveyard and I couldn't scream, run or cry. As a couple of minutes passed until I was greeted by Mr. Taliban. First impression he was young like we were close in age. I felt relieved, Thank God some one like me. He's a young man I started feeling good about everything again I was ready for this job. My first week was interesting I was teamed with a female carrier that been there for years. Every morning before she left she would case all the mail. There were tubs, and trays of mail. There was mail everywhere. The part of the job that I was interested in was being on the street. I wanted to feel apart of society. This was what it was about being away from the graveyard into life. However, this part was the hardest part. All I kept thinking about was the stories you hear of dog attacks. Therefore, I was on a look out. However, to me the only thing attacking me was the mail. It was horrendous traveling from mailbox to mailbox. I was so tired sometimes I just wanted to stop and go home. However, giving up was not an option. While this job proved itself to be challenging, I continued to keep the faith and keep moving. On some routes, some people did not have mail slots; there were these never-ending steps. Sometimes I would climb up twenty or more steps just to put in one piece of mail. There were times I wanted to just stop drop and roll. Due to my feet aching. Well with thoughts of stopping only kept me pushing on. It was tough but I knew that if I kept moving it would all work it self out.

STOP CIRCLING
COMPLETE CIRCLES

After examination of the years before I can't help but to see I been going in complete circles. I want out I needed to get out. I'm so dizzy I need to be revived. How did I make it this far. The circle started with the Post Office then in the middle of the circle here comes the CNA which lead me back to the Post Office. That was not the end still circling back to being a CNA which then lead me back to the Post Office for a mail carrier position. Where was the logic in all of this for me circling. While circling I knew that I was done. No more dealing with this mail service. I just wanted to go back to being a customer. I was done with trying to be a CNA and a psychiatrist . I never remember that being apart of the job description. At this point I had to turn it over to God. It was time to say good-bye. I just had to keep them in my prays while I 'm praying for my sanity. In the beginning I did not know that it would be the biggest circle of my life. Remembering the Bubble Boy I had no idea that I would be left feeling like the Bubble Girl. This circling did not just involve jobs also people in my life as well. Well for starters this is where anything with solidity will ever last. First recognizing, understanding, Cherishing, and loving your relationship with the higher power. See a long time ago down memory lane we all stumbled on a rock that said this is not about you. But we as humans, just as ignorant and dumb as we can sometimes choose to be chose to ignore the sign. Well I'm here to say Hey stop ignoring the signs and get into your higher power. Let that be your everything before anything else. See it's not about where you think you're going it's about where you know you're going. So when you know your higher power is directing your paths you know enough to shut up and listen. Ok it was a process before I could unveil this truth. I stumbled on many of rocks along my paths. For many of my years on earth I ignored these signs. Okay after stumbling, and falling so many times. I had to examine what I was doing wrong. In my mind and perception I was trying my hardest to do everything right. However I had to stumble and fall many of times to get up and realize that was just a figment of my imagination. Sometimes I would look back and say maybe I did not have to experience that or that if I would have only listen to my higher power. I guess just like everyone else that think they can do it their way I was only deceiving myself. It then came a time when my deception was so weary that all it brought was weary days. From this job to that job all for what. No money left to say hey I gave you this many years of my life and I have zero dollars. I mean I needed a way out this madness. I just knew it was going to be difficult. However it may have come with challenges, but it also comes with its fulfillment. Nothing else on earth can be fulfilling unless it's a purposeful life with the higher power. I may not know everything, but my higher power does and I believe as long as I stay close to him as time go on it will be revealed what I did not know.

I was living a life of death. I wanted a happiness that would not go away with the lost of a job or with the lost of money. I wanted an eternal happiness. Therefore, in my submissiveness of the truth I was granted my happiness. However, with my happiness their was still questions in my mind that lingered around. I wanted to know the full truth. I needed answers, so on my quest for these answers I knew that I was in for the revelations. Well I turned to the one person that I knew had information to give. My mother, I know she had answers and I was all ears. So as I proceeded with my answer quest. With unsurely of what was going to be discovered. Well for starters my mother never fully was able to enjoy her youth because of the responsibilities of a young mother. The negative emotions that come along with being a young mother from family as well as strangers. In my mother time, the right thing at the time to do was to be married before a child was brought in to the situation. My mother shared with me there was so much pressure on her to marry the father of her unborn child at the time. If not the consequence was no communication or visiting privileges. With the information that was provided about my mother herself. I wanted to go deeper, It was time to know my Grandmother. I have no memories of my late Grandmother. The only memory I have is a shared memory of me being present in the hospital room before she died. However, I do not remember my mother told that to me. So as my mom talks about my late grandmother she always express that her mother suffered so much emotionally. Because of her childhood. The first fact my grandmother mother died when she was a young girl. She was the oldest girl, so she carried so many responsibilities. As I listened to these stories of her , I see and feel the challenges. So as time went on and she tried to conduct a life with four children including my mother, life just was too challenging. My mother expressed how her mother would be gone for weeks leaving my mother and her siblings with no food no money. My mother remembers her mother always at the bars. I guess doing what so many people do try to mask their emotions, challenges, pain, and fears with substances. Their have been reports through the family my late grandmother was sexually abused. My grandmother so vulnerable from a youngster with the death of her mother at 30 yrs of age, and later her father suffered from a nervous breakdown. Well from all of the information I received there was pieces to the puzzle put together. My mother always said, "She never wanted to be like her mother." Well I was saddened to know the truth that she was like her mother. For one she never tried to nuture her children gifts or learn her children. My mother's, mom did not never care to know who she was. For two I never seen my mom do drugs or consume alcohol, however I always seen my mom spend so much money on clothes and jewelry so excessively. So here there was clear evidence that even though it may not been 100 percent identical. It was real enough to know there was simarilarities. As my conclusion fill in many pieces. Now I was challenge with breaking this cycle ending the sickness, healing the wounded. I know that I was being used for that through God.

THE DISCOVERY
& RECOVERY

Iknew there had to be a reason for me being a kind hearted person. The reason was there clear that people need to feel God's love. I "Aaliyah Zakat" am God's love. Now I was ready everything was becoming more and more clear about just who God bless me to be. I was excited and thrill about everything my future was shining bright and I was walking into it. My time had arrived and I could not want or needed more that what I did. I would spend the rest of my month collecting on positive thought ideas and positive interactions that would start a new beginning for world peace. As months pass I had ups and downs. I still was challenged however I knew it was a new beginning. That alone, was my motivation for the journey. My journey of God. So much my life I was stuck on this victimized lifestyle, that I wanted a new character. I was a new character and God was in the director's chair. It was time for me to play my position. Who was I to fight or disagree with God and what God wanted for my life? Once I knew this truth I was willing, however I know it is going to be challenging. I realized that anything worth having is worth fighting for. Especially when God assign something for you. I had good days and I had very challenging days. When I had challenging days I would just hold so tight on the blessings of God. I always knew I was so blessed, so I would hold on everything that God blessed me with while challenged with the negative. I knew that my prior lifestyle was not working. I was not clear everything that God wanted to do with me. I did know I was exhausted and I needed a new life. I did know that what God had for me was going to take complete faith. I knew that it was out of my hands. It was all in God's hands and I was relieved. Now I felt like why did I wait so long. So now I was conflicted with the fact that I took so long. However I knew that in any fashion way or form that I was going to be greatly challenged in which I was. I knew that my battles was not mine own, I surrendered my whole being to God. So I was battled with taking myself completely out of it. It sounded easier than it actually was. On a constant basis I had to tell myself that it was in God's hands. In addition, what helped me to let go knew that with me following and being submissive to God that whatever happens God is got me. So when I was challenged with my daughter growing up being apart of people in this world. Her being among good and bad. Sometimes just the thought would make me cry. Me being a survivor of abuse, me knowing the affects, troubling thoughts, poor choices lack of self worth that it can bring. I started to get so stressed just thinking about it or just the look in my daughters eyes would saddened me. That's when God said just surrender this battle is not yours. God shared with me that what you don't want to happen to your daughter, that there are children going through abuse daily. God was saying what are you going to do to try to help the youth period. Here God gave me the solution. It was pure truth. At this point of wanting to just give up because of the challenging thoughts God gave me the solution. Well I knew I was done feeling incompetent. I wanted to strengthened myself as well as my daughter. So it was the right thing to do is to try to be involved.

Aaliyah Zakat

9-1-08   MY ROAD TO SUCCESS

Upon leaving my house I was greeted by a neighbor saying these few words that would delight me in my travel. He forwardly commented that every time he see me I look like sunshine. I accepted the comment with my signature smile and continued with my journey. All my life I received pleasant compliments however these comments was so different from all my struggles I face within my fleshly being. I always felt like I could put on a great smile,but on the other hand I felt as no one gets me. People don't get the full understanding of just who AALIYAH ZAKAT is. To God I am a vessel for and from him . To Humans I am as complicated as it gets. However Gods let me know it is A okay. This road I 'm on can be very challenging the God in me give me the strength ,the courage the joy the peace the endurance, the discipline, the control the faith the mindset of sincerity that I need on my journey. God knows me . Even when I may go a little off the right path God knows whats in my heart and God knows where my heart is. I am just human .I read so situations where others deal with the same feelings that I feel. However I never had the opportunity I feel like to have a face to face with a young woman just as me who feel what I feel know what I know been where I been. However I want that person to stand tall against hate

,stupidity ignorance and self doubt. These people stories that I come across majority of these story tellers fell for drugs. God has bless me to deal with good and the bad and never once did drugs. I am so thankful for that .I can't imagine something taking over me other than my one and only God. On the other hand I can sympathize with former drug abusers. The feeling of the pressure from taking on all the emotions that come from occurances in life that feel out of your control. I feel like it is okay to be Cool listen to your favorite music doing your favorite thing,but also remembering that stuff is temporary to go far and farther than you could ever dream about you need solidity something solid. The next day 9-2-08 I typed on my computer I sent some emails I knew that I could not stay in the house so I got me and my daughter prepared for the evening of our travel. My daughter is always willing to go where ever mommy is going. We traveled to the bookstore Borders , while there we ate the crunchy herr's pretzels. I also packed some hawaiann punch for my daughter thirst. After the pretzels and the juice my daughter could not be contained. Earlier while she had her snack she was calm afterwards she wanted to play all around the book store. Me as a willing person I let her play. My daughter given a inch of freedom and she'll take a mile. I remember myself being that way. I wanted to be free I wanted to do what I wanted to do when I wanted to do it. Then I carried on my life like I was unstoppable. Me being a witness to my daughter traits that can work for her or against her. I know early on that the only way it can work for her is keeping God first . Also I know that I would be the tool that God will use to assure that. I feel so much pressure for 1 this is my first child so I am a newby in the mother department. God always let me know that I am doing a good job. THANK YOU GOD FOR THAT. I LOVE YOU. MAY GOD KEEP ASSURING ME THAT I AM DOING THE RIGHT THING DESPITE WHAT PEOPLE THINK,SAY,OR DO IT'S NOT ABOUT THEM IT'S ABOUT GOD IT'S ABOUT GOD. I LOVE YOU. When I started to see how so many things that is done can work against you. I knew that a God has to exist there so many negative things that can play with your mental, rape your flesh and expose and dispose your flesh. I said to my self this is where God comes in to make everything better to pick you up from guilt,shame, sadness, crys, pains, and abuse I said this is were God comes in and makes it okay. God just comes in and say It is okay. When you have people with no hope around you saying with out saying damn how is she ever going to recover from that one and that one and that one saying now how is she going to recover from that abuse. Then you hear the words from God saying you're doing good when you have God showing you more than all of the doubters can ever see all together even with the biggest telescope that man could ever make. God show you all possibilities when these people see only the impossible. God visions are the greatest in the world when the picture in front look so hopeless. God given me vision so far to Japan to every country I never been to every thing I always wanted back then but did not know how to attain it God gave me that vision for every thing I may have always wanted. God given me everything my being could ever have wanted, or needed from a child. I Aaliyah Zakat is a living testimony All Things Are Possible With God. Amen ! To me it seemed when I was challenged I did not know where God was in my life. Now I lived to realize it was me that strayed away from God. So I now see how all my life I have been distracted from my God. So now it's clear to me just how satan work. I realized how manipulative, coniving the devil can be. So God bless me with the freedom, God freed me from the blindness to the devil. With the new light God gave me clarity. Now I see there was nothing wrong to serve God. God is our stability in a unstable world with unstable people. Even when the devil may encourage you can do it by yourself. We will only fool ourselves in results crawling back to God. When we accept where not in control are ourselves. Because frankly we don't know how to be. We need God continuously to help us. As long as where deceived to believe, we can achieve life absence of God. It only hurts and frustrates are time on earth. Just think of the people that came before you, what things they left earth feeling like they should have accomplish. We will never know, but God will always know. I believe that can be an uneasy feeling to understand something when you're out of time. We think we know who we are however God knows who we are. Nothing is more rewarding than doing God's work.

Printed in the United States
By Bookmasters